Are we fucking or no?

In Loving Memory of Kim Luttrell-Roshcell, my loud, proud friend
July 17, 1965–September 25, 2021
—L. C.-R.

To loud little girls who speak up when something needs to be said,
and to their sisters, who encourage them to scream louder
—K. J.

SIMON & SCHUSTER BOOKS FOR YOUNG READERS
An imprint of Simon & Schuster Children's Publishing Division
1230 Avenue of the Americas, New York, New York 10020
Text © 2023 by Lesa Cline-Ransome
Illustration © 2023 by Kaylani Juanita McCard
Book design by Laurent Linn © 2023 by Simon & Schuster, Inc.
SIMON & SCHUSTER BOOKS FOR YOUNG READERS and related marks are trademarks of Simon & Schuster, Inc.
For information about special discounts for bulk purchases, please contact Simon & Schuster Special Sales
at 1-866-506-1949 or business@simonandschuster.com.
The Simon & Schuster Speakers Bureau can bring authors to your live event. For more information or to book an event,
contact the Simon & Schuster Speakers Bureau at 1-866-248-3049 or visit our website at www.simonspeakers.com.
The text for this book was set in Caecilia LT Std.
The illustrations for this book were rendered digitally.
Manufactured in China
0523 SCP
First Edition
2 4 6 8 10 9 7 5 3 1
Library of Congress Cataloging-in-Publication Data
Names: Cline-Ransome, Lesa, author. | Juanita, Kaylani, illustrator.
Title: Loud and proud : the life of Congresswoman Shirley Chisholm / Lesa
Cline-Ransome ; illustrated by Kaylani Juanita.
Description: First edition. | New York : Simon & Schuster Books for Young Readers, [2023] | "A Paula Wiseman Book." | Includes bibliographical references. |
Audience: Ages 4–8 | Audience: Grades 2–3 | Summary: "Shirley Chisholm (1924–2005) is a hero and trailblazer. She was the first African American woman
in Congress (1968) and the first woman and African American to seek the nomination for president of the United States from one of the two major
political parties (1972). Written by award-winning author Lesa Cline-Ransome, here is her story"—Provided by publisher.
Identifiers: LCCN 2022001740 (print) | LCCN 2022001741 (ebook) | ISBN 9781534463523 (hardcover) | ISBN 9781534463530 (ebook)
Subjects: LCSH: Chisholm, Shirley, 1924–2005—Juvenile literature. | African American legislators—Biography—Juvenile literature. | Women legislators—
United States—Biography—Juvenile literature. | Legislators—United States—Biography—Juvenile literature. | United States. Congress. House—Biography—
Juvenile literature. | African American presidential candidates—Biography—Juvenile literature. | Women presidential candidates—United States—
Biography—Juvenile literature. | Presidential candidates—United States—Biography—Juvenile literature. | Brooklyn (New York, N.Y.)—Biography—Juvenile
literature. | New York (N.Y.)—Biography—Juvenile literature.
Classification: LCC E840.8.C48 C55 2022 (print) | LCC E840.8.C48 (ebook)
| DDC 328.73/092 [B]—dc23/eng/20220126
LC record available at https://lccn.loc.gov/2022001740
LC ebook record available at https://lccn.loc.gov/2022001741

LOUD and PROUD

The Life of Congresswoman
Shirley Chisholm

Written by
Lesa Cline-Ransome

Illustrated by
Kaylani Juanita

A Paula Wiseman Book
Simon & Schuster Books for Young Readers
New York London Toronto Sydney New Delhi

Shirley Anita St. Hill was always small, but she talked big, walked tall, and told just about everyone what to do.
  "Bossy" is what her family called her. And bossy is what she was.

In Brooklyn, New York, her parents, Charles and Ruby St. Hill, sewed and cleaned, cooked and fixed, scraped and saved. Tucked in tight with her three sisters in one bed, her parents in another, Shirley learned that all the love in the world couldn't pay for heat or a better apartment or parents who didn't have to labor for hours on end to fill their bellies.

At night, through the thin walls of their apartment, Shirley
listened to the heated voices of her father and his union friends as
they shouted about jobs and fairness, opportunities and politics.

During the day, her father read in the newspaper the words of activist Marcus Garvey and President Franklin D. Roosevelt, men whose plans and policies gave him pride and gave him hope.

Shirley sat by his side, first listening, then talking till her voice was as loud as her father's. Both were looking for answers in a world that seemed to turn its back on people who had less.

"Here come the St. Hill girls!" neighbors would announce as Shirley led her younger sisters up and down city blocks. Even in their homemade dresses of fabric scraps, all four held their heads high to church and to school, the only places their parents allowed them to go. Each had a Bible, a dictionary, and a library card.

"God gave you a brain; use it," their father demanded.

So, at Girls' High School on Nostrand Avenue, Shirley became the vice president of the Honor Society.

"Too intellectual" was what her classmates called her. And intellectual is what she was.

On a full scholarship to Brooklyn College, Shirley joined the Political Science Society, the debate club, and the National Association for the Advancement of Colored People (NAACP); she volunteered for the Urban League; and she started her own club for black women.

"Always talking about some big, serious thing" was what the other students said about her. And she was.

But Shirley talked over classmates who laughed and doubted her.

When her political science professor told her, "You ought to go into politics," Shirley paid attention.

First she painted posters. Then she wrote speeches and organized rallies and campaigns for her female classmates who were denied a role in campus politics.

Shirley graduated, started teaching, finished graduate school, and married Conrad Chisholm, but the more Shirley worked in politics, the more she could see how the people in her community were made to feel small every day. Treated unfairly in education, housing, and jobs. No one was out fighting for them, so Shirley took the lead.

In 1960 Shirley helped to form the Unity Democratic Club and rang doorbells and got her neighbors to voting booths to make their voices heard. In 1964, when a seat for the New York State Assembly opened up, Shirley decided it was her turn.

But first she needed four thousand signatures on a petition to get her name on the ballot. One by one, Shirley knocked on doors, but some people weren't happy to see a black woman asking for their vote.

"What are you doing running for office?" they asked.

"Go home to your husband," they scoffed.

"Be quiet!" they screamed.

Shirley knew she was making noises people didn't like. But Shirley didn't listen to words that made her feel small. Especially when she was fighting for something big.

Shirley got all the signatures she needed and more and won the race with nearly 90 percent of the vote.

In the capital city of Albany, where the New York State Assembly convened, Shirley was only the second black woman to hold the seat for the Seventeenth Congressional District. She passed into law eight bills that helped students from poor neighborhoods attend college and gave unemployment insurance to those who cooked and cleaned, scraped and saved.

Four years later Shirley ran for Congress.

As she campaigned in Brooklyn housing projects, her voice blared from speakers, "Ladies and gentlemen, this is Fighting Shirley Chisholm coming through." She talked loud about paying for day care and college, and she talked proud about having money for food and rent.

"I have no intention of being quiet," she said.

"Go home. You don't belong here," men told her.

So Shirley knocked on the doors of women, sat at their kitchen tables, bounced their children on her knee. She attended PTA meetings and church services. She listened to the voices of mothers and maids, students and secretaries. Women who needed day care they could afford and good-paying jobs and apartments with heat for the winter. And then she asked them, "Can you help me?"

Women turned up and turned out. They handed her coins and dollar bills from money raised at bingo parties and bake sales. They showed up at voting booths. They sent Shirley out of Brooklyn, down Route 95 to the nation's capital in Washington, DC, and into the ninety-first session of the United States Congress.

"There may be some fireworks," she told her supporters.

Her fellow congressmen didn't know what to make of the first black congresswoman on Capitol Hill.

"What does your husband think of all of this?" one asked her.

Unlike her male colleagues, Shirley had an all-female staff running her congressional office. She worked around the clock attending House sessions and committee meetings in the chamber.

When congressional leadership tried to quiet Shirley by putting the New York City native on the Agricultural Committee, Shirley loudly fought for a food stamp program.

When they told her to slow down, Shirley worked quickly to secure money for the Head Start early education program. When they told her to remember her place, Shirley made her own place by helping young students get work through Job Corps.

"If they don't give you a seat at the table, bring a folding chair," she said.

Shirley waited for other women and black leaders to stand tall and use their voice in politics. But during her second term in Congress, Shirley got tired of waiting and stepped forward for everyone who needed a loud, proud voice fighting for them.

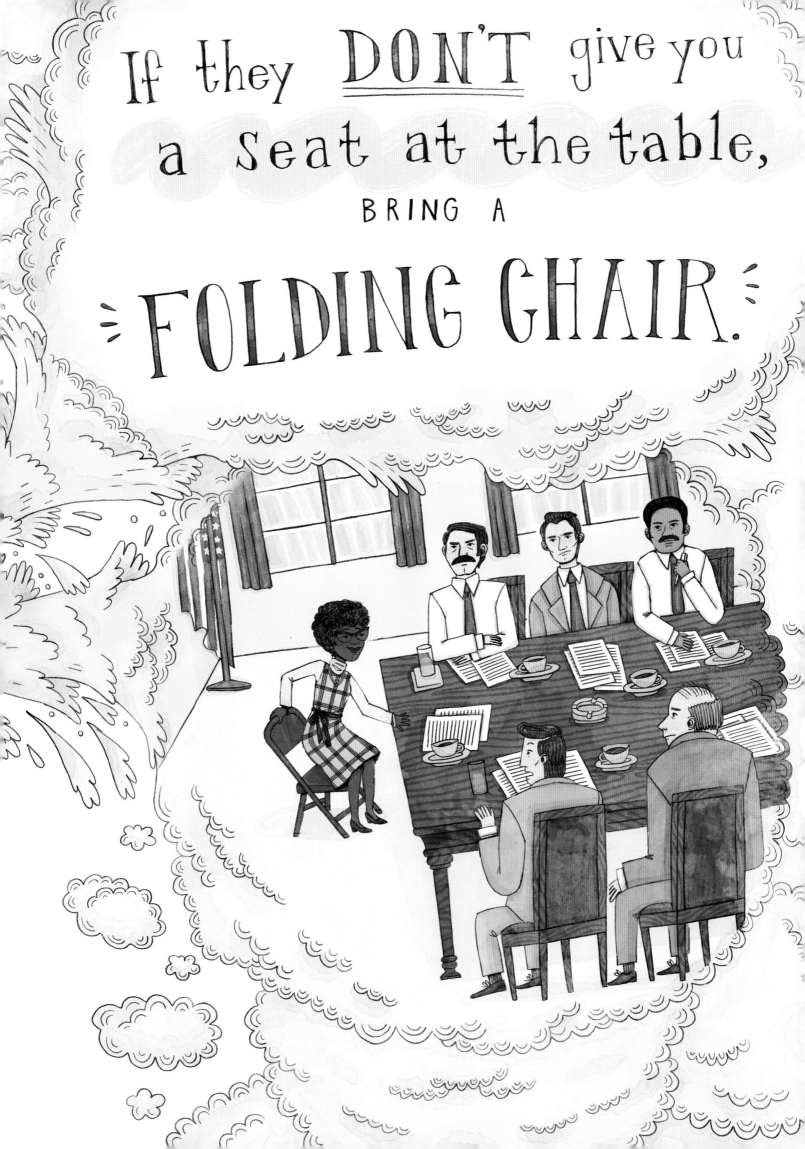

HUMPHREY HUBERT

ED MUSKIE

GEORGE WALLACE

GEORGE McGOVERN

SHIRLEY CHISHOLM

RICHARD NIXON

JOHN G. SCHMITZ

LINDA JENNESS

BENJAMIN SPOCK

LOUIS FISHER

WILBUR MILLS

JOHN HOSPERS

In 1972, as the race for the U.S. presidency began, twelve candidates announced they were running against the incumbent Republican president, Richard Nixon. In a field of mayors and senators, governors and representatives, not one of the candidates looked like Shirley.

From the pulpit of the Concord Baptist Church in Brooklyn on January 25, 1972, Shirley stood tall as reporters jostled with their notebooks and cameras.

Echoed through the microphone, Shirley's speech began: "I stand before you today as a candidate for the Democratic nomination for the presidency of the United States of America."

Cameras popped. "I am not the candidate of black America, although I am black and proud."

I AM THE CANDIDATE of the PEOPLE of America!

Pencils scribbled. "I am not the candidate of the women's movement of this country, although I am a woman and I'm equally proud of that," Shirley preached. "I am the candidate of the people of America!"

Roars of applause rang out from the church pews.

Shirley wasn't sure she could raise enough money to fund a campaign. Shirley wasn't sure she would get enough votes. But Shirley was sure she had to try. "I am supposed to be seen and not heard. But my voice will be heard."

Up and down the country, Shirley campaigned against poverty, the Vietnam War, racial discrimination, and inequality. Shirley's supporters followed her on the "Chisholm Trail," proudly wearing her "Unbought and Unbossed" campaign slogan buttons fastened to their lapels.

CHISHOLM
READY OR NOT

CHISHOLM TRAIL

CHISHOLM
PRESIDENT FOR THE PEOPLE

TA
THE
CHIS
TRAI
TO
160
P

"If you can't support me, if you can't endorse me, get out of my way," Shirley told those who disagreed with her candidacy.

GET OUT OF MY WAY.

When the campaign ended, Shirley had earned over four hundred thousand votes and finished ahead of nearly half the other candidates in the Democratic primary. Shirley may have lost the race for the presidency, but she was just getting started.

Back in Congress, Shirley returned with a voice louder than ever.

As a founding member of the Congressional Black Caucus and the Congressional Women's Caucus and the only woman on the powerful House Rules Committee, Shirley continued her fight for affordable childcare, funding for education, and amendments to the National School Lunch Act.

And then, in 1983, after seven terms in Congress, Shirley stepped aside, leaving politics behind to allow other women to move ahead on the path she'd paved for them.

"I want to be remembered as a catalyst for change in America,"
Shirley said, loud and proud for the world to hear.

BARBARA JORDAN

CHARLENE MITCHELL

MAXINE WATERS

SHEILA JACKSON LEE

AYANNA PRESSLEY

PETA LINDSAY

KAMALA HARRIS

ILHAN OMAR

ALEXANDRIA OCASIO-CORTEZ

★ ★ ★ ★ ★ AUTHOR'S NOTE ★ ★ ★ ★ ★

"My little Shirley Chisholm" is what my mother used to call me when I was at my most strong-willed as a child. I never knew if she intended the statement as a compliment, but that is how I took it. Images of Shirley Chisholm on television and in newspapers showed a proud black woman, uncowed by convention. She was everything I wanted to be. Like Shirley, "bossy" is what my family called me. And bossy is what I was.

Born on November 30, 1924, to immigrant parents from Guyana and Barbados, Shirley Chisholm spent seven terms in the United States House of Representatives. When she began her first term in 1968, she was the very first black female congressperson in the U.S. House of Representatives. While in Congress, Shirley introduced more than fifty pieces of legislation, focusing her attention on issues that impacted women, children, and underserved communities as well as ending the Vietnam War. She also sponsored increases in federal funding to extend hours of day care facilities, backed an expanded national school lunch program, and supported federal assistance for education.

I was seven years old in 1972, the year Shirley Chisholm ran for president of the United States. At home I listened to the music of the Jackson 5, the Isley Brothers, Bill Withers, Al Green, and Curtis Mayfield: the soundtrack of the struggles and triumphs of the black community. In 1969 James Brown's "Say It Loud, I'm Black and I'm Proud" became the de facto black national anthem during the post–civil rights movement. Shirley Chisholm was the embodiment of loud and proud.

Shirley emerged on the political scene during the convergence of the black pride and women's liberation movements, yet she received lukewarm endorsements from both. It was, in large part, younger black college students and black women who formed the foundation of her campaign and provided a groundswell of grassroots support. The Black Panther Party political organization often conducted her voter registration drives and fund-raisers. Future congresswoman Barbara Lee was an early campaign worker and delegate during Shirley's presidential campaign.

Shirley's "Unbought and Unbossed" campaign slogan represented a new brand of politics that refused to accept financial contributions from donors who demanded political favors in return. Shirley was a proud product of the working class who reminded voters, "Don't sell that vote out."

United States Representative Shirley Chisholm announces her entry for Democratic nomination for the presidency at Concord Baptist Church in Brooklyn, New York.

Her presidential run was initially not taken seriously by the media or political rivals. She was blocked from participating in the televised presidential debate until she successfully sued for the right to appear alongside her rivals. She entered twelve primaries and, despite having an underfinanced campaign, managed to earn 10 percent of the delegates to the Democratic primary meeting, where the party's candidate would be decided.

When Shirley returned to Congress after her presidential bid, she was appointed to the powerful House Rules Committee, which oversees how bills are introduced through the House.

Shirley Chisholm retired from Congress in 1983. She went on to teach at Mount Holyoke College in Massachusetts. She was offered the ambassadorship to Jamaica but declined due to poor health. In 2005 she passed away in Florida.

Her legacy continues to live on through her legislative accomplishments. President Barack Obama posthumously awarded her the Presidential Medal of Freedom in 2015. In his speech at the ceremony he said, "There are people in our country's history who don't look left or right; they just look straight ahead. And Shirley Chisholm was one of those people."

In 2019 the 407-acre Shirley Chisholm State Park opened in New York.

Democratic representative Ayanna Pressley of Massachusetts, the current occupant of Shirley Chisholm's former office in the Longworth House Building, said of the former congresswoman, "The vibe of her office fills me with the courage to boldly lead, boldly legislate, and to never forget those who sent me here."

Shirley became a congresswoman at a time when women serving in Congress were a rarity, let alone black women. Today, there are 102. Over one third of them are women of color.

THE CHISHOLM TRAIL ★ ★ ★ ★

1924 • Shirley Chisholm is born in Brooklyn, New York, to Charles St. Hill and Ruby Seale

1928 • Shirley is sent to Barbados with sisters Muriel and Odessa to live with her maternal grandmother to allow her parents to work and save money

1934 • Shirley and her sisters return to Brooklyn; a new sister, Selma, is born

1936 • Family moves to Ralph Avenue in Brooklyn; Shirley attends Junior High School 178

1942 • Graduates from Girls' High School in Brooklyn

1946 • Graduates from Brooklyn College

1949 • Marries Conrad Chisholm

1951 • Earns a master's degree in early childhood education

1960 • Forms the Unity Democratic Club (along with five others) to reform Brooklyn politics and run more candidates of color in local campaigns

1964 • Elected to New York State Assembly (and won reelection twice, in 1965 and 1966)

1968 • Elected to United States Congress

1971 • Founding member of the National Women's Political Caucus and the Congressional Black Caucus; began serving on the Education and Labor Committee

1972 • Launches her historic presidential campaign

1983 • Retires from Congress

2005 • Shirley Chisholm passed away at her home in Ormond Beach, Florida